STARTING POINT

—

Leader Guide

This journal belongs to:

Dynamic Catholic

Design by Doug Beyer, Ben West, and Ashley Wirfel

ISBN: 978-1-63582-129-1

FIRST EDITION

10   9   8   7   6   5   4   3   2   1

People don't care how much you know until they know how much you care.

A Brief Letter to Session Leaders

Meeting Parents Where They Are . . .

. . . And leading them to where God is calling them to be.

Baptism is a beautiful, life-giving sacrament. It's also a unique opportunity.

Some parents will be all in from day one. They know the Catechism, they never miss a holy day of obligation, and they are thirsty for the theology behind Baptism.

But many of the parents you'll encounter will not be so eager or willing to dive in. Many rarely attend Mass. These parents might be getting their child baptized out of obligation to a family member or because they themselves were baptized. ("That's just what you do, right? It can't hurt.")

But they did just have a baby. Their world was turned upside down—we know that much. They are ready to ask the big questions. They are open to hearing big answers. They are feeling what we at Dynamic Catholic call the "sacred stirring"—the desire to seek a-better-version-of-themselves, to live for more, to dream. This is our opportunity to help show them God has big dreams for their family.

Starting Point

A Different Kind of Baptismal Preparation

Baptism is about initiation, not obligation. Initiation into God's family and the Church, and initiation into the best way to live. Baptism is the first step of the great life God desires for each of us. And it is unique because infant Baptism, in many ways, is almost as much about the parents as it is about the child—the parents are the ones taking the vows, after all. What a gift! Parents willingly give their child over to God for heavenly adoption!

This is why STARTING POINT focuses on the parents.

STARTING POINT: *Helping Parents Raise Great Children* is a Baptism preparation program and parenting resource with three main objectives: (1) inspire parents to start discovering the dreams they have for their child, their marriage, and their family; (2) invite parents to explore all the ways God and the Church can help them fulfill these dreams; and (3) encourage parents to understand and maximize their influence during the nine years in which they are the primary influencers of their child's life and beliefs.

To best accomplish these objectives, STARTING POINT consists of two parts: the in-person parent session and the guided dream journal experience (*A Parent's Journal for Dreaming*), which parents will do together at home on their own time.

Thank You!

Helping parents raise amazing children is the greatest thing we can do for God's kingdom. Thank you for your passion, your dedication, and your collaboration. Thank you for all you are doing for the Church.

A thriving, dynamic parish must have thriving, dynamic parents. Parents are the first catechists of a child—they accept this responsibility at their child's Baptism—but they are the first evangelizers too. A family is only as strong as its parents; a parish is only as strong as its families. Words could never fully express just how important this work is. Thank you!

May the grace of our abundantly generous God inspire you and give you courage, wisdom, and patience.

For thousands
of years God
has been using
ordinary
people to do
extraordinary
things.

Preparing for the In-Person Parent Session

Watch the videos beforehand and review the listed discussion questions.

Familiarize yourself with the guided dream journal (*A Parent's Journal for Dreaming*) you'll be giving to couples (one journal per couple).

It's important that you have a dream journal to give each couple because it is used for both the in-person parent session and the guided dream journal experience.

As a gesture of welcoming hospitality, we recommend you serve snacks and offer coffee (new parents are often tired or simply in need of a little TLC).

NOTE: The suggested format is one 45 to 60 minute session with the parents in which you and they will watch videos, discuss topics, and ask questions. However, the program is flexible and can be adapted to fit your particular parish or diocesan needs—whether that is filling a single two-hour session (allowing more time for discussion between videos) or multiple sessions (e.g., watching and discussing one video per session).

Look at your students. Each one of them is Jesus in disguise.

LEADING THE PARENT SESSION

 Instructions + Guided Dream Journal (5 min.)

When they arrive, thank the couple(s) for being there and hand them the gift of the guided dream journal (*A Parent's Journal for Dreaming*). Let them know that this is a free gift from the parish to use as a resource for their parenting and to help them discover their dreams for their child. Also let them know that they will be using the journal to answer questions during the session with you.

Spend some time getting to know each other. If you are hosting more than one couple, it will be helpful to have name tags so they can get to know each other and begin to feel like they have some new friends in the parish community. Keep the focus of the conversation on the parents, with questions such as: How are you handling parenthood? What's been good? What's been surprising? What's been challenging?

2 Opening Prayer (2 min.)

God our Father,

We thank you for the gift of children
and your gift of Baptism. We praise you for
being the ultimate example of parental love.
And we ask that you open our hearts and
inspire our minds so that we may
imitate your perfect example—
so that we may love our children l
ike you love us.

Help us to choose the-best-version-of-ourselves
each day as we learn to parent,
not without mistakes but without regrets.

Please, we pray, walk with us
during this journey, and give us the strength
and wisdom to seek your counsel above all else,
so that our children may come to know
and love you too.

Amen.

3   Explain the Format (3 min.)

This session will consist of three short videos. The guided dream journal provides questions and space for couples to write down their answers (and any questions of their own) while watching the video or during the discussion afterward.

TIP: Encourage the fathers to write in the journal
so they are engaged and feel more involved
(plus, Mom might have a hungry baby on her hands!).

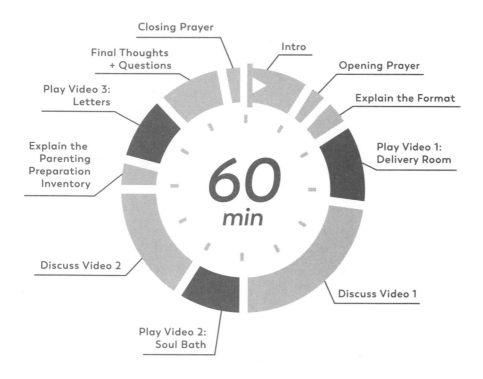

Closing Prayer

Final Thoughts
+ Questions

Intro

Opening Prayer

Play Video 3:
Letters

Explain the Format

Explain the
Parenting
Preparation
Inventory

Play Video 1:
Delivery Room

60 min

Discuss Video 2

Discuss Video 1

Play Video 2:
Soul Bath

Delivery Room

4 **Play Video 1: Delivery Room** (5 min.)

The first video is a bit of a surprising and comedic journey, but it has a very clear and powerful message for new parents. We recommend that you try not to set the film up too much. Just let them experience it for themselves. It is designed to disarm parents, giving them something they are not used to seeing from the Church, especially as it pertains to sacramental preparation. Encourage parents to write in the guided dream journal if they have thoughts or questions while watching (page 31).

5 **Discuss Video 1** (15 min.)

Writing down their dreams is the most important part of this section. Make sure you give them at least five minutes to write. Remind them that if they get stuck, there are dream prompts in their dream journal.

Dream Writing Session

Give the parents five minutes to write down as many dreams as possible.

Dream Prompts

· If you could go on one dream trip with your family, what would it be?

· What kinds of spiritual habits would you like to establish?

· Do you want physical fitness or healthy diets to be important to your family?

· What will you do to encourage learning outside school?

· Will your children know the importance of saving money?

· Are there any traditions you want to establish around holidays, birthdays, and other important days?

· Describe the character of the man or woman you would like your child to marry—or the man or woman you want your child to become when he or she is twenty-five.

Discussion Questions

· What surprised you most about this video or the dream writing session?

· Was it easy or difficult to think of dreams for your family?

· Under what category do most of your dreams fit (financial, spiritual, educational, etc.)? What categories seem lacking?

Soul Bath

6   **Play Video 2: Soul Bath** (5 min.)

The second video is all about Baptism—the day of, what is worn, what is said, what is happening, and why. The video will clearly walk parents through what they will be doing and what to expect at the baptism. As you discuss the video, Soul Bath, with the parents, it may be helpful for you to point them toward pages 102-103 and 106-107 of their Dream Journals for exactly what you will be asking them to do and to say at the baptism. This can help build their confidence and expectations for what will be happening during the sacrament. Encourage parents to write in the guided dream journal if they have thoughts or questions while watching (page 109).

7   **Discuss Video 2** (10 min.)

We have provided a few prompt questions to help spark conversation after the video, but we recommend that you give parents plenty of time to ask their own questions first during this time.

Understand,
many of these people
may have never
discussed Baptism in
their life.

Discussion Questions

- What part (or parts) of Baptism excites you most? Why?

- What does it mean to you for your child to be adopted by God? Have you ever considered that this is what happens at Baptism?

- Think of your godparents. Have they had an active role in your faith formation?

- How important is it to you that your child's godparents are active in his or her life?

- What can you do to ensure the godparents are as involved as you would like?

8   Parenting Preparation Inventory (5 min.)

Take a break from the videos and discussion to talk about the Parenting Preparation Inventory and remind couples to complete the inventory on their own time.

There is nothing else like this in the world. It was developed in partnership with the renowned Catholic psychologist Dr. Gregory Bottaro, to get parents thinking and, more importantly, talking about parenting styles and situations. This will spark conversations that would otherwise rarely come up, and it is essential for parents to experience.

You can find more information and the link to the inventory on page 54 of the guided dream journal.

TIP: Remind parents that there are no right or wrong answers. This is about sparking great parenting conversations, ensuring parents are on the same page, and fortifying marriages and strong parenting teams.

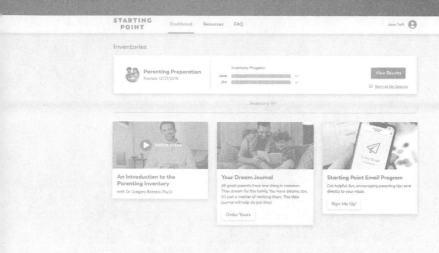

Inventory Questions

To gauge where parents agree and disagree

Dive deeper into each topic

with psychologist
Dr. Gregory Bottarro

Letters

9 **Play Video 3: Letters** (5 min.)

The third video will encourage and inspire parents. People don't do anything until they are inspired, but once they are inspired there is almost nothing they won't do. Encourage parents to write their thoughts and reactions in the guided dream journal (page 117).

Discussion questions and a letter-writing exercise are provided in the dream journal for parents to complete on their own time (page XX), but the class is designed to end here—sending them home on a positive note!

10 Final Thoughts and Questions (5 min.)

Take a moment to thank the couple(s) again. Ask if there are any closing questions.

Encourage parents to begin reading and using their guided dream journal (*A Parent's Journal for Dreaming*). Part two of the journal contains all the Baptism information covered in the video and more.

Remind them to take the Parenting Preparation Inventory (page 54).

Let them know that the videos they watched today can be found online (the dream journal contains the links to them as well).

Ask parents to sign up for the STARTING POINT email program (or help them sign up on their phones during the session). When they sign up, they will receive helpful free parenting tips twice per week. They can sign up at DynamicCatholic.com/ParentingTips.

11 Closing Prayer (2 min.)

Lord our God,

We ask that you bless these parents
as they prepare for their child's Baptism.
Give them the grace and wisdom to fully experience this
powerful sacrament, and help them become
the amazing parents you created them to be.
Teach them to dream.

We ask that you bless all the influencers
in this child's life—friends, teachers, godparents, siblings,
mentors, and coaches—that they might be positive
and loving, always guiding this child
toward truth and happiness.

And we ask that you bless this child.
Thank you for the opportunity to welcome
a new member into your family, the Church.

We ask this in the name of the Father
and of the Son and of the Holy Spirit.

Amen

Let the little children come to me, and do not hinder them, for the kingdom of God belongs to such as these.

Matthew 19:14

For the day we accept that we have chosen to choose our choices is the day we cast off the shackles of victimhood and are set free to pursue the lives **we were born to live.**

Matthew Kelly

NOTES

- **Parents' Names:**

  ....

  ....

- **Child's Name:**

  ....

  ....

- **Baptism Date:**

  ....

  ....

NOTES:

Reflections:

What do you want to remember about this child and his or her family?

....

....

....

....

....

....

What is God saying to you through your encounter with this child and his or her family?

....

....

....

....

....

....

- **Parents' Names:**

  ....

  ....

- **Child's Name:**

  ....

  ....

- **Baptism Date:**

  ....

  ....

  NOTES:

Reflections:

What do you want to remember about this child and his or her family?

....

....

....

....

....

What is God saying to you through your encounter with this child and his or her family?

....

....

....

....

....

....

- **Parents' Names:**

  ....

  ....

- **Child's Name:**

  ....

  ....

- **Baptism Date:**

  ....

  ....

NOTES:

Reflections:

What do you want to remember about this child and his or her family?

....

....

....

....

....

What is God saying to you through your encounter with this child and his
or her family?

....

....

....

....

....

- **Parents' Names:**

  ....

  ....

- **Child's Name:**

  ....

  ....

- **Baptism Date:**

  ....

  ....

  NOTES:

Reflections:

What do you want to remember about this child and his or her family?

....

....

....

....

....

....

What is God saying to you through your encounter with this child and his or her family?

....

....

....

....

....

....

- **Parents' Names:**

  ....

  ....

- **Child's Name:**

  ....

  ....

- **Baptism Date:**

  ....

  ....

  NOTES:

Reflections:

What do you want to remember about this child and his or her family?

....

....

....

....

....

What is God saying to you through your encounter with this child and his or her family?

....

....

....

....

....

....

- **Parents' Names:**

  ....

  ....

- **Child's Name:**

  ....

  ....

- **Baptism Date:**

  ....

  ....

  NOTES:

Reflections:

What do you want to remember about this child and his or her family?

....

....

....

....

....

....

What is God saying to you through your encounter with this child and his or her family?

....

....

....

....

....

....

- **Parents' Names:**

....

....

- **Child's Name:**

....

....

- **Baptism Date:**

....

....

NOTES:

Reflections:

What do you want to remember about this child and his or her family?

....

....

....

....

....

What is God saying to you through your encounter with this child and his or her family?

....

....

....

....

....

- **Parents' Names:**

....

....

- **Child's Name:**

....

....

- **Baptism Date:**

....

....

NOTES:

Reflections:

What do you want to remember about this child and his or her family?

....

....

....

....

....

....

What is God saying to you through your encounter with this child and his or her family?

....

....

....

....

....

....

- **Parents' Names:**

  ....

  ....

- **Child's Name:**

  ....

  ....

- **Baptism Date:**

  ....

  ....

  NOTES:

Reflections:

What do you want to remember about this child and his or her family?

....

....

....

....

What is God saying to you through your encounter with this child and his or her family?

....

....

....

God never goes back; he always moves forward . . . God always wants our future to be bigger than our past.

MATTHEW KELLY

- **Parents' Names:**

  ....

  ....

- **Child's Name:**

  ....

  ....

- **Baptism Date:**

  ....

  ....

  NOTES:

Reflections:

What do you want to remember about this child and his or her family?

....

....

....

....

....

What is God saying to you through your encounter with this child and his or her family?

....

....

....

....

....

....

- **Parents' Names:**

....

....

- **Child's Name:**

....

....

- **Baptism Date:**

....

....

NOTES:

Reflections:

What do you want to remember about this child and his or her family?

....

....

....

....

....

....

What is God saying to you through your encounter with this child and his or her family?

....

....

....

....

....

....

- **Parents' Names:**

  ....

  ....

- **Child's Name:**

  ....

  ....

- **Baptism Date:**

  ....

  ....

  NOTES:

Reflections:

What do you want to remember about this child and his or her family?

....

....

....

....

....

What is God saying to you through your encounter with this child and his or her family?

....

....

....

....

....

....

- **Parents' Names:**

....

....

- **Child's Name:**

....

....

- **Baptism Date:**

....

....

NOTES:

Reflections:

What do you want to remember about this child and his or her family?

....

....

....

....

....

....

What is God saying to you through your encounter with this child and his or her family?

....

....

....

....

....

....

....

- **Parents' Names:**

  ....

  ....

- **Child's Name:**

  ....

  ....

- **Baptism Date:**

  ....

  ....

NOTES:

Reflections:

What do you want to remember about this child and his or her family?

....

....

....

....

What is God saying to you through your encounter with this child and his or her family?

....

....

....

....

God, grant me the serenity to accept the things I cannot change; courage to change the things I can; and wisdom to know the difference.

Amen.

REINHOLD NIEBUHR

- **Parents' Names:**

....

....

- **Child's Name:**

....

....

- **Baptism Date:**

....

....

NOTES:

Reflections:

What do you want to remember about this child and his or her family?

. . . .

. . . .

. . . .

. . . .

. . . .

What is God saying to you through your encounter with this child and his or her family?

. . . .

. . . .

. . . .

. . . .

. . . .

. . . .

- **Parents' Names:**

  ....

  ....

- **Child's Name:**

  ....

  ....

- **Baptism Date:**

  ....

  ....

  NOTES:

Reflections:

What do you want to remember about this child and his or her family?

....

....

....

....

....

What is God saying to you through your encounter with this child and his or her family?

....

....

....

....

....

....

- **Parents' Names:**

....

....

- **Child's Name:**

....

....

- **Baptism Date:**

....

....

NOTES:

Reflections:

What do you want to remember about this child and his or her family?

....

....

....

....

....

....

What is God saying to you through your encounter with this child and his or her family?

....

....

....

....

....

....

....

- **Parents' Names:**

  ....

  ....

- **Child's Name:**

  ....

  ....

- **Baptism Date:**

  ....

  ....

NOTES:

Reflections:

What do you want to remember about this child and his or her family?

What is God saying to you through your encounter with this child and his or her family?

- **Parents' Names:**

....

....

- **Child's Name:**

....

....

- **Baptism Date:**

....

....

NOTES:

Reflections:

What do you want to remember about this child and his or her family?

....

....

....

....

What is God saying to you through your encounter with this child and his or her family?

....

....

....

Don't worry that children
never listen to you;
worry that they are always watching you.

ROBERT FULGHUM

- **Parents' Names:**

  ....

  ....

- **Child's Name:**

  ....

  ....

- **Baptism Date:**

  ....

  ....

  NOTES:

Reflections:

What do you want to remember about this child and his or her family?

....

....

....

....

....

....

What is God saying to you through your encounter with this child and his or her family?

....

....

....

....

....

....

- **Parents' Names:**

  ....

  ....

- **Child's Name:**

  ....

  ....

- **Baptism Date:**

  ....

  ....

  NOTES:

Reflections:

What do you want to remember about this child and his or her family?

....

....

....

....

....

What is God saying to you through your encounter with this child and his or her family?

....

....

....

....

....

....

- **Parents' Names:**

  ....

  ....

- **Child's Name:**

  ....

  ....

- **Baptism Date:**

  ....

  ....

  NOTES:

Reflections:

What do you want to remember about this child and his or her family?

....

....

....

....

....

What is God saying to you through your encounter with this child and his or her family?

....

....

....

....

....

....

- **Parents' Names:**

....

....

- **Child's Name:**

....

....

- **Baptism Date:**

....

....

NOTES:

Reflections:

What do you want to remember about this child and his or her family?

....

....

....

....

....

....

What is God saying to you through your encounter with this child and his or her family?

....

....

....

....

....

....

- **Parents' Names:**

  ....

  ....

- **Child's Name:**

  ....

  ....

- **Baptism Date:**

  ....

  ....

NOTES:

Reflections:

What do you want to remember about this child and his or her family?

....

....

....

....

What is God saying to you through your encounter with this child and his
or her family?

....

....

....

*The greatest trick the devil ever pulled was
convincing the world he didn't exist.*

UNKNOWN

- **Parents' Names:**

  ....

  ....

- **Child's Name:**

  ....

  ....

- **Baptism Date:**

  ....

  ....

  NOTES:

Reflections:

What do you want to remember about this child and his or her family?

....

....

....

....

....

What is God saying to you through your encounter with this child and his or her family?

....

....

....

....

....

....

- **Parents' Names:**

  ....

  ....

- **Child's Name:**

  ....

  ....

- **Baptism Date:**

  ....

  ....

  NOTES:

Reflections:

What do you want to remember about this child and his or her family?

....

....

....

....

....

What is God saying to you through your encounter with this child and his or her family?

....

....

....

....

....

....

- **Parents' Names:**

....

....

- **Child's Name:**

....

....

- **Baptism Date:**

....

....

NOTES:

Reflections:

What do you want to remember about this child and his or her family?

....

....

....

....

....

What is God saying to you through your encounter with this child and his or her family?

....

....

....

....

....

....

- **Parents' Names:**

  ....

  ....

- **Child's Name:**

  ....

  ....

- **Baptism Date:**

  ....

  ....

NOTES:

Reflections:

What do you want to remember about this child and his or her family?

....

....

....

....

....

....

What is God saying to you through your encounter with this child and his or her family?

....

....

....

....

....

....

- **Parents' Names:**

  ....

  ....

- **Child's Name:**

  ....

  ....

- **Baptism Date:**

  ....

  ....

  NOTES:

Reflections:

What do you want to remember about this child and his or her family?

....

....

....

....

What is God saying to you through your encounter with this child and his or her family?

....

....

....

A little child has no difficulty in loving, has no obstacles to love. And that is why Jesus said: "Unless you become like little children you cannot enter the kingdom of God."

MOTHER TERESA

- **Parents' Names:**

....

....

- **Child's Name:**

....

....

- **Baptism Date:**

....

....

NOTES:

Reflections:

What do you want to remember about this child and his or her family?

....

....

....

....

....

....

What is God saying to you through your encounter with this child and his or her family?

....

....

....

....

....

....

- **Parents' Names:**

  ....

  ....

- **Child's Name:**

  ....

  ....

- **Baptism Date:**

  ....

  ....

  NOTES:

Reflections:

What do you want to remember about this child and his or her family?

....

....

....

....

....

What is God saying to you through your encounter with this child and his or her family?

....

....

....

....

....

- **Parents' Names:**

  ....

  ....

- **Child's Name:**

  ....

  ....

- **Baptism Date:**

  ....

  ....

  NOTES:

Reflections:

What do you want to remember about this child and his or her family?

....

....

....

....

....

....

What is God saying to you through your encounter with this child and his or her family?

....

....

....

....

....

....

- **Parents' Names:**

....

....

- **Child's Name:**

....

....

- **Baptism Date:**

....

....

NOTES:

Reflections:

What do you want to remember about this child and his or her family?

....

....

....

....

....

....

What is God saying to you through your encounter with this child and his or her family?

....

....

....

....

....

....

- **Parents' Names:**

  ....

  ....

- **Child's Name:**

  ....

  ....

- **Baptism Date:**

  ....

  ....

  NOTES:

Reflections:

What do you want to remember about this child and his or her family?

....

....

....

....

What is God saying to you through your encounter with this child and his or her family?

....

....

....

The most extraordinary thing in the world is an ordinary man and an ordinary woman and their ordinary children.

GK CHESTERTON

- **Parents' Names:**

  ....

  ....

- **Child's Name:**

  ....

  ....

- **Baptism Date:**

  ....

  ....

  NOTES:

Reflections:

What do you want to remember about this child and his or her family?

....

....

....

....

....

....

What is God saying to you through your encounter with this child and his or her family?

....

....

....

....

....

....

- **Parents' Names:**

  ....

  ....

- **Child's Name:**

  ....

  ....

- **Baptism Date:**

  ....

  ....

NOTES:

Reflections:

What do you want to remember about this child and his or her family?

What is God saying to you through your encounter with this child and his or her family?

- **Parents' Names:**

....

....

- **Child's Name:**

....

....

- **Baptism Date:**

....

....

NOTES:

Reflections:

What do you want to remember about this child and his or her family?

What is God saying to you through your encounter with this child and his or her family?

- **Parents' Names:**

  ....

  ....

- **Child's Name:**

  ....

  ....

- **Baptism Date:**

  ....

  ....

NOTES:

Reflections:

What do you want to remember about this child and his or her family?

....

....

....

....

....

....

What is God saying to you through your encounter with this child and his or her family?

....

....

....

....

....

....

- **Parents' Names:**

  ....

  ....

- **Child's Name:**

  ....

  ....

- **Baptism Date:**

  ....

  ....

NOTES:

Reflections:

What do you want to remember about this child and his or her family?

....

....

....

....

What is God saying to you through your encounter with this child and his or her family?

....

....

....

Remember that nothing is small in the eyes of God. Do all that you do with love.

SAINT THERESE OF LISIEUX

- **Parents' Names:**

  ....

  ....

- **Child's Name:**

  ....

  ....

- **Baptism Date:**

  ....

  ....

  NOTES:

Reflections:

What do you want to remember about this child and his or her family?

....

....

....

....

....

....

What is God saying to you through your encounter with this child and his or her family?

....

....

....

....

....

....

- **Parents' Names:**

....

....

- **Child's Name:**

....

....

- **Baptism Date:**

....

....

NOTES:

Reflections:

What do you want to remember about this child and his or her family?

What is God saying to you through your encounter with this child and his or her family?

- **Parents' Names:**

  ....

  ....

- **Child's Name:**

  ....

  ....

- **Baptism Date:**

  ....

  ....

  NOTES:

Reflections:

What do you want to remember about this child and his or her family?

....

....

....

....

....

What is God saying to you through your encounter with this child and his or her family?

....

....

....

....

....

....

- **Parents' Names:**

....

....

- **Child's Name:**

....

....

- **Baptism Date:**

....

....

NOTES:

Reflections:

What do you want to remember about this child and his or her family?

....

....

....

....

....

What is God saying to you through your encounter with this child and his or her family?

....

....

....

....

....

....

- **Parents' Names:**

  ....

  ....

- **Child's Name:**

  ....

  ....

- **Baptism Date:**

  ....

  ....

  NOTES:

Reflections:

What do you want to remember about this child and his or her family?

....

....

....

....

What is God saying to you through your encounter with this child and his or her family?

....

....

....

*Love begins at home,
and it is not how much we do... but how much
love we put in that action.*

MOTHER TERESA

- **Parents' Names:**

  ....

  ....

- **Child's Name:**

  ....

  ....

- **Baptism Date:**

  ....

  ....

NOTES:

Reflections:

What do you want to remember about this child and his or her family?

....

....

....

....

....

What is God saying to you through your encounter with this child and his or her family?

....

....

....

....

....

....

- **Parents' Names:**

....

....

- **Child's Name:**

....

....

- **Baptism Date:**

....

....

NOTES:

Reflections:

What do you want to remember about this child and his or her family?

....

....

....

....

....

....

What is God saying to you through your encounter with this child and his or her family?

....

....

....

....

....

....

I AM THE *son*
OF A GREAT **KING.**
He is my father
AND MY GOD.
THE WORLD MAY PRAISE ME
OR CRITICIZE ME.

IT MATTERS NOT.

HE IS WITH ME,
always at my side,
GUIDING AND PROTECTING ME.

I DO NOT FEAR
because
I AM HIS.

I AM THE *daughter*
OF A GREAT **KING.**
He is my father
AND MY GOD.
THE WORLD MAY PRAISE ME
OR CRITICIZE ME.

IT MATTERS NOT.

HE IS WITH ME,
always at my side,
GUIDING AND PROTECTING ME.
I DO NOT FEAR
because
I AM HIS.

Better
TOGETHER

MARRIAGE PREPARATION AND ENRICHMENT

Helping Couples Create Great Marriages

We know you're passionate about preparing couples to
experience the incredible marriage God has planned for them.
But we also know that every couple you meet with is coming from
a different level of engagement with their faith. That's why we
created BETTER TOGETHER, a marriage prep program that meets
couples where they are and equips them to build lasting,
happy, and faith-filled marriages.

Visit DynamicCatholic.com/Better-Together
to get your free program pack.
(Just pay shipping)

HAVE YOU EVER
WONDERED HOW THE
CATHOLIC FAITH
COULD HELP YOU
LIVE BETTER?

How it could help you find more *joy* at work, *manage* your personal finances, *improve* your marriage, or make you a *better* parent?

THERE IS GENIUS IN CATHOLICISM.

When *Catholicism* is lived as it is intended to be, it elevates every part of our lives. It may sound simple, but they say *genius is taking something complex and making it simple.*

Dynamic Catholic started with a dream: to help ordinary people discover the *genius of Catholicism.*

Wherever you are in your journey, we want to meet you there and walk with you, *step by step*, helping you to discover God and become *the-best-version-of-yourself.*

To find more helpful resources, visit us online at DynamicCatholic.com.

 **Dynamic Catholic**

FEED YOUR SOUL.